Moonsoulchild:

The Journey Through My Heart

You're not **dumb** to **love someone** with **all** your **heart**,
To want someone who is *no good* for you.

People with good hearts have the most trouble with this; we see the best in people and expect them to see the same in us. You can't make someone love you. That's why it's essential to not wait around for someone who won't ever love you. For the ones who wake up one day and decide they no longer love you, let them go. Let them go the second they give you that sign. Knowing they couldn't be straightforward from the beginning. A reminder, no response doesn't mean there's hope. There's no need to attach crazy ideas that love will revisit like the first time you fell in love with them. Don't let them come back, time and time again, while they left you without wonder. You don't deserve to wait around for love; that's unclear, undecided, and gone.

You're not wrong to **ghost** people,
especially if you've *explained* yourself **repeatedly**.

We all have a story about how someone hurt us; we reflect on everyone we meet, expecting them to understand, hoping they won't hurt us the same. But, unfortunately, everyone won't be right for you, and sadly, you must let those people go. The more you chase someone who doesn't want to be chased, you'll find yourself in the same situation. If you feel there isn't anything left to say you don't need to explain yourself. If you do decide to explain why you let them go, be prepared not to get the answers or the apology you want. Be obliged to approach with an open mind, not a heavy heart. Use your heart less, or you'll be asking to destroy yourself.

Losing someone is one of the most *complex* parts of life.

It doesn't matter how; it will hurt. The worst part about letting go is you'll still love them. It's crazy how our hearts can continue loving someone who only brings pain. You were meant to love everyone who walked in your life; it's impossible to analyze every connection you created, but when it's over, you'll feel it. There's nothing that will ease the pain; what's gone is gone. Don't drown yourself in pain that no longer serves its purpose. The longer you hold onto it, the longer you'll go without finding it again.

Roadblock

Same **beginning**,
same **ending**
I'm immune to it
I know nothing different.
I'm scared to admit
this is the end.
If it is,
promise me
you won't pretend.

The **pain** will always make you feel like nothing.

It takes time to heal wounds that are still fresh. It doesn't matter how long it lasted; if you have a good heart, the way you love will always feel difficult, and the pain will always feel unbearable. *You must let yourself feel everything*; and know; you can either feel the heartache forever or try to find **happiness** in places it does exist.

I'm all about giving **second** chances,

Then there comes a time when you have no more chances left to give. Taking the same people back after the first time doesn't feel the same. The more you allow, the more they'll keep doing it. Sometimes we love the thought of love and attach it to someone because we want to love. It's hard to know when love's real. I don't believe in second chances when it comes to real pain, repeatedly. I believe it takes time to understand the pain you feel, which makes it hard to let go. You'll never let the one who's meant for you find you if you keep running back to them. The one thing about toxic people, they'll swear to love you but leave you and then want you back. They can't have you and everything else they want. You're hurting yourself more by sticking around than letting go.

People always told me **love wasn't real**.

It's sad how bitter some can be when it comes to someone else being happy. How someone can no longer care they forget about everything you once shared. I've never been bitter, only blind. The hardest thing is being sure even though you know in your heart it's wrong; you want so badly for it to be right. I've learned, as much as you want something, you can't make something that's not meant for you, meant for you. You can't force anything; it will destroy you. I thought I had loved all figured out until I found out heartbreak is real. Once you fall in love, there are no limits; there are no rules. You're in it; you either give your all or watch it go. Suddenly, that love was taken from you by someone you once said those three words to. To love someone, you must always have your guard up. To love someone, you must think positively but never forget the bad times. To love someone gives you faith when someone says they'll never break your heart; always keep in mind they still could. To love someone, you must know heartbreak is real. As easy as it's to love, it's easier to hate. To me, love has always been beautiful. I also learned the person you love might not be. When someone told me love wasn't real, I looked at them, smiled, and replied, trust me, it's real.

I've crossed so many paths,
met many different people,
yet everyone I come across
seems to have the same ways.
"I love you"
I just can't stay.
Same old game
one I'll never win.

I thought loving and caring
unconditionally was important
I didn't realize
It was a way to be taken for granted;
to be used for someone else's advantage.

It's <u>not their job to heal me</u>,
they shouldn't need to do time
for someone else's crime.
It's hard to love someone else
without the word **pain**
crossing every line
and the word *trust*
being erased from my mind.

<u>Lost goodbyes</u>

I wish we didn't get close
only to get distant.
I wish before we fell,
we would have *guarded our hearts*
at all costs.
I wish before we got distant
we could have made it known.

To **love yourself,**

It takes a lot of heartbreak and losing people you thought you'd never live without. It causes you to lose yourself, realizing there's no one you need more than yourself. **Don't rush the process**; *don't set comfort* in places you need to work to be happy.

<u>Your heart isn't a weapon.</u>

Being heartless isn't something to be proud of; it's not something to show off. Being heartless means hiding from the most amazing thing you could ever experience, love. Don't hide from love but don't go out looking for it either. **Let love find you.** Let yourself feel everything you feel. Your most incredible power is to feel every single emotion. You either accept it or go through your whole life being heartless, not knowing the true meaning and the best parts of life.

Differences

You can have a different mindset from someone and still accept their differences. Even if you'd choose the opposite, that's the beauty in love.

Don't change

You can be the rawest version of yourself; some people will always see you how they see you. When it comes down to it, those are their issues. Don't let *how they deal* with their **insecurities** *make you change*.

People will pick apart your flaws
to discover your weaknesses.
They'll use their insecurities
to try and make their **flaws** *invisible*
without realizing,
their <u>insecurities shine brighter</u>.

They don't define your beauty

You were beautiful before them, while you were with them, and now. They don't define your beauty. Your beauty is deeper than what meets the eye. Think about your heart, how you love and how you show that love openly That's your **authentic** beauty, *don't let anyone take that from you.*

This time around, no second chances

Many of us attach love to someone we want to love and end up with nothing close to what we deserve. Making someone love you doesn't work, and if it does, it will always be flawed in a way the pain won't ever let you see brighter days. Every day will feel like a challenge of making the other person happy. Don't waste time that can be pursued in other areas. It's hard for big hearts to let go; we must be honest with them this time, **no second chances**.

The unknown

No one will just leave out of nowhere; **there's always a reason**. They'll know, but you won't. People don't wake up one day and decide they don't want you anymore; they've thought of leaving ways. That's why I believe sometimes no answer is the answer people find most comfort in. knowing they don't need to explain how they feel or why they left; they would instead move on and forget it happened. There was love, but love wasn't enough to keep things that weren't meant to go on. **Love is strong** but sometimes *not enough* when it comes to endings; when it's over, it's over. If you go, you'll feel like you'll never know what could happen. If you're scared, if you go back, nothing will be the same; it won't; it will always feel foreign. Change isn't something you'd want, and right now, you're giving them the power.

You can't identify someone by what they wear or the things they decide to have. There are reasons why there are millions of the same things. *Those things weren't meant to define you.* The only thing that can define you is your heart.

There's no heart like yours,
the way you love,
the way you **show your heart**.
That's <u>different</u>,
that's **special**.

Sometimes we get caught up in how we feel and forget the other person's feelings and what they want. *We create an illusion* of what we want; then sometimes others have a way of making us love them, just to leave us like your nothing and lead us somewhere you can't explain the feeling. You can't make someone like you; whether it's your physical beauty or your inner beauty, neither change when it comes to them; how they see you, how they feel about you is their perception.

You'll always be beautiful,
your heart will always be pure.
Don't let dark times dim your beauty.

The **saddest** part of <u>letting go,</u>

The **memories always remain**; seeing them will instantly make you remember every emotion you felt when you left things; it doesn't mean it's real. It's important to know how to *separate your heart from the memories*.

There wasn't much I could do to save connections with people who only gave me reasons to walk away. **I tried** to love them despite how hard they made it. I tried accepting our differences and separated our hearts further apart, but *I decided to save myself instead.*

The pain they brought upon you is no longer holding you from happiness; *you're happier now without them.* Remember everything they put your heart through and start accepting it **wasn't your loss**; it was <u>theirs</u>.

I found my balance

I've had days where happiness feels endless
some feel like happiness is out of reach.
Without both,
I couldn't find my **balance**,
I wouldn't have known
there are better days.
I always tried fixing what was lost
Instead of creating happiness
In everything I did.

No more lost connections

I'm not interested in being **liked**, *understood*, or **accepted**. Those don't determine my worth. I live in a world filled with people who always try to make me into someone I don't recognize. I'm *not interested* in making any more **lost connections**.

I hope you *don't take this wrong,*

Just because you believe they're your soulmate isn't a reason to stick around. If they are truly your soulmate, let them go, and the universe will bring you back together if it's meant to be. The more you try and fight what's already written, the unhappier you both will be. I believe in the timing of all, I believe that people can be right together, but the timing can be wrong. I also believe in the signs people show; if they keep repeating the same mistakes and treating you like you're not worth an explanation, they're showing you their worth doesn't amount to yours. We all believe someone is our soulmate when we love them; we fight for them even when we shouldn't need to. You shouldn't need to make someone see how much you love them; they should feel it. Love is not enough to hold together a broken bond. Sometimes, people let go emotionally and hold onto you physically because they won't want you to find the one you're meant for; they believe holding you back will always keep you. Sometimes, you must **let go** and see what's meant to happen or who is **meant** for you out there.

Struggling with your emotions

You can't feel one emotion for the rest of your life; that's why it's important not to hoard the same old emotions and old pain. Accept you can't change anyone. Sometimes, we need to let go of who we love for reasons that will never make sense. Sometimes it's nothing more than they aren't meant to serve you anymore purpose; **let the demons** go along with them.

<u>Finding yourself</u>

There's nothing wrong with wanting to explore the world and who you are as a person without someone else. It's natural to want to see what and whos out there for you. It's unfair to hold someone close to you when you know you can't give them what they need. It's not fair to love someone from afar, but sometimes we have no choice. When you love someone, experiencing life with them is the first thing you'll want; at that point, you will be sure of a foundation for who you are. If you haven't got there, **find yourself**, it's the *most important step of it all*.

Let me tell you,

People stick around 99% of the time because they would rather be **mistreated than be lonely**. You'll tend to find comfort in being by yourself and loving your own company. Right now, you're accepting disrespect from someone you keep letting walk all over you, not understanding it's because you keep letting them. You know they're no good yet can't understand why you never leave. The longer you stick around, the more pain you feel when it's over. There's nothing good that comes out of a connection that only makes you think of ways out. You can love someone wrong for you; your heart was meant to love people in your life for many reasons, but we're also meant to let the same people go for reasons you'll never completely understand. The universe is giving you signs on why to leave; follow them. There's **no real love** in someone who *breaks your heart* over and over and **watches you pick up the pieces**.

Not everyone is meant for you,

There will be some who will only hurt you because that's the role they were meant to play in your life. So don't try to rewrite the story and change it. Loving people who *don't deserve* your love will only **drown you in darkness**.

"What you *convinced* your **heart** was **real**."

While you focus on who you left behind or trying to leave behind, there's someone out there waiting to find you, while you're giving your love to someone who doesn't deserve it. Find *the love that feeds your soul*, not the version of the love you convinced your heart was genuine.

If you have a big heart,

You're considered **weak**.
Having no heart is the trend,
having a good heart is dangerous
knowing you could break at anytime
and still,
give your **all**.
There's *nothing weak about you*.

I stopped accepting the love that was only conditional and beneficial. I stopped accepting the love that was only love when it was desired. I withdrew from people when I unfolded, my love became a **secret** from the world, and my *downfall* became their success.

Don't be a second option

I never understood someone who had someone wonderful before them and still chose to walk a different path. I never understood why someone could just let someone amazing slip through their fingers, why someone would let you fall in love with them, just to hold you to the side while you watch them love someone else. People don't know how to have someone good do good by them. Sometimes relationships can be toxic, along with friendships and any connection. You weren't meant to have a longer path with them; you served your purpose. There's no revisiting what once was, it's gone, and that's a sign right there that you shouldn't be the only one holding on for good purpose while they're just keeping you around to be their **second option**.

When you meet someone who you instantly fall in love with, you'll feel nothing you felt before. It's easy to fall in love, especially with someone good at faking. I learned a lot about love and relationships, even friendships, to know that *toxic people have a way* of showing you all their good and hiding the side of someone you've never seen. You need to accept that's who they are and who they always were. You can't tell yourself how they feel, nor will you ever get the answer directly from them. Toxic people will always be toxic to people they weren't meant to be with. The more you keep fighting this, the more pain you bring upon yourself and drown in it. Toxic people have a way with words, and they're also good at showing you nothing at all. The *universe will never* match you with **someone hard to love**. If it's that hard to be with someone, you reached your road, and it's time to move on.

You'll always continue the **same patterns** with *toxic* people; they'll swear they'll change, and you end up questioning why you thought it was possible to keep trying to save them. You don't have the strength to *keep giving* your **energy** away and your **heart** so easily.

It's like everything you once thought was real is now something you can't explain to anyone because it just wouldn't make sense. Don't ever feel ashamed of who you love and why you love them. They weren't meant to grow with you and who you're going to be one day because who they are right now will never be who they'll be. You will overanalyze why people left, was it you, or was it them. The truth is, it doesn't matter who's at fault; you'll be thankful you let go one day. You'll be grateful for being let go of. Sometimes we can't let people go because we use love as an excuse not to see the dishonest love and silent judgments of people who give up so quickly. You'll learn they never loved you as much as they said; people don't just walk out of your life when they love you. I believe that **connections you can't save were meant to break**. You don't think about letting people go when you meet them when you fall in love with them. If you analyzed every connection you made, a mess would be made.

    I believe you cross paths with people meant to show us a part of us we didn't know was there. The kind that felt love in letting go and letting people we once loved, free and *becoming a better you.*

You must **love your own company** before sharing your company with anyone. You don't need to always be the need of everyone and don't feel bad for taking time for yourself. You can't keep others happy when you're draining yourself.

We all have days where we have setbacks; days we don't feel we can go on longer. The thing about it is you'll always make it. Your mind has a way of making you believe you can't handle pain. The way to start the **healing process** is to let go of trying to fight how you feel; you need to feel everything entirely and understand why things happen, but don't over-analyze to the point it drives you crazy. There will be things you won't understand for good reasons. What plays out was already planned; you don't know **your fate** *until it's in front of you.*

It's crazy,
you were raised to love people closely
and suddenly,
you grow up to learn
not *everyone*
was raised like you.
Some make it hard
to love them,
so **you end up**
loving them from afar.

If you ever wondered why
I never gave you *all of me*,
Ask yourself why
I promise you'll find your answer there.

Don't let someone change your heart.
Don't let them take advantage either.
Forgive for yourself
and your growth,
the **grudges** you hold onto
will only *kill you slowly*.

Watch who you ask about me,
There's some
That used to love me
That will *never be honest about who I am.*
To them,
I'll always be **misunderstood**.
To them,
I'll always be wrong.

I want to be loved in a way
It won't *hurt*
and I won't need to worry.
Because I,
will be everything I am
and that will be **enough**.

We can walk the same streets,
follow the same signs
and still not make it to each other.
We can **pour our hearts out**
and tell each other what's on our minds,
and still not make it through to each other.
We could talk for hours
and tell each other
how much we love another
and still not understand
why we bother.

The **sad part of loving someone** is the memories will always be there, no matter the situation or timing; seeing them will instantly make you remember, and you will feel it, every emotion you last left things. That doesn't mean it's real. You let go and left it all behind you. Don't let it control you into thinking they have control over you. When you see them, remember the reasons you left and where you're at now, and compare the differences in why you decided to leave. Keep remembering until you're no longer mad, upset, or sad. You'll be able to look at them and smile, wishing them the best because the pain they brought upon you is no longer holding you from happiness. You're happier now without them, and you need to remember that. Remember, there's no point in *holding onto grudges that only affect you in the end*. So the next time you see them, look at them; you'll remember everything intensely and feel nothing.

People will **fake** it
until they get it
and try to *make you into the fool.*

Selfish

From giving all of me,
to always love more.
I don't regret it
but there's no chance
you'd catch me a second time
giving all of me
to someone,
who took more than they could give.

If *loving my own company*
meant **letting go of souls**
who didn't fight to stay,
being in my own company
is *where I'd choose,*
every time.

After all this time,
I've been mistaken
like everything we built up
Is crashing.
I have been hurt before
but this,
might break me.

I **promise** that your trust,
your secrets
and all of your dreams.
Most importantly,
your heart is safe with me.

"I want to breathe"

The **past** that haunts me,
the past that needs to die.
I don't want the memories,
let them die,
let them leave.
I want to forget them,
I want to breathe.

Don't waste your time on who doesn't value you.
Your time is too precious
to be **wasted** on people
who give you nothing in return.

Self-love is frightening these days,
They would rather be **you**.

You don't need to make sense to anyone; you don't owe anything to anyone. You can be someone; someone doesn't understand. There is a *treasure in being different*; you don't need to be understood; you can be yourself.

Being happy is more important than making sense to someone who only needs validation.

It doesn't matter how **loyal** you are or the lengths you would go to for someone. If they don't love themselves, they can't give you the love you need. *Stop draining your heart* of **love that can't be given back to you**.

I can't believe
I ever thought
loving myself was *selfish*.

I found us **falling apart**, to the point where I ended up doing me, pushing them into the direction of not needing them. When at the end of the day, *their love was all I wanted.*

I stopped trying to find the missing pieces
to **broken connections.**
My love shouldn't be a mystery,
my worth shouldn't be a game.

Love is real, but sometimes people make it painful and challenging. *Promises can be broken* every day. I no longer believe in love, a least *the love I thought was real*. No one should give up but always keep your guard up. Because well, **heartbreak is real**.

I will be the person I am, and if someone doesn't like me, they can forget me. If someone can't love me the way I want to be loved, in better words, the way I deserve to be loved, *I refuse to give my heart away*. No matter how long it takes, I won't let anything break me, every obstacle I will get through. Being happy with myself is the key to it all. I will no longer cry over what's not mine and instead be happy about the things I have. The universe took people and things out of my life for a reason. Not many can say they deserve the best because we all accept the things we think we deserve.

Life is too hard to understand; it's also too short to analyze. Don't spend too much time on something you know might never last, but don't give up on something if you believe in your heart is real. Accept that people change, things change, and sometimes nothing stays the same. Sometimes you need to let go. So many people don't know who they are, but **I've grown to understand me**.

Loving yourself *isn't* days full of happiness; some will be amazing, and some will be terrible. Some you won't recall, and some you won't forget. The love you feel for everyone you meet will be beautiful. You'll accept nontoxic forming connections while knowing your worth. You won't accept people who want to drag you through their negative habits. Accept you can't change things, and you will grow into someone you won't recognize, but you'll love it.

You'll finally feel **comfortable being yourself**.

I'm sorry you got let down, time after time,

And you couldn't figure out why you stayed. Love is so confusing sometimes; it confuses you into thinking just because you love someone, you should have them in your life when you shouldn't. The more you force them to stick around, the more they'll want to go. I feel sometimes people may love you but be terrified to love all of you because they can't be free anymore, and it's sad; there's so much beauty in being free with someone you love. Love for them will always be there, but it doesn't mean you need to be there. You don't need to put all or half of yourself into anything that keeps destroying you.
I've learned not to let them upset me into thinking that *the version they see me will become my reality.*

I was scared to be someone *without them,*
to not need them
and not cater to their **toxic** needs.
There was no need for me to be around people
who only wanted to use me
to love themselves more.

Free write

The patience and time I put into every *heartbreaking* decision broke me up until I had nothing left. Knowing I could have done something different, but I didn't know until the end. I pretended when a new person came along, new struggles also came. When reality hit, they were the same heartbreaking struggles I was left with from the beginning. I guess this is what you call being alone; the happiness never seemed to stay strong.

I tried to be **happy**
But it has been a long run,
I just can't keep up.

When you love someone, you love them. Your whole soul loves them without thinking twice. It doesn't matter the relationship, **love is love**, and the people you love will be important in your life. Just like you were meant to meet people, you were meant to tell someone you thought you'd never need to let go. There are many paths out there; some people can't decide which road to take, and when they do, you may not take the same one. Don't let anyone make you feel the way you choose to grow is wrong, and who you are is someone unfamiliar. No one can identify you as someone you're not. Who you are will always be authentic when you give your heart, especially to people who only give their time.

Accept the *good* in **goodbyes**
Like you appreciate the first glace,
Both tie into *how you find yourself.*

Many ask you,
"what's **wrong**"
And not accept
"*I don't know*" for an answer.
Like there's no such thing
as not knowing,
as if they *never once felt alone.*

You are **strong**
You are *amazing*
You are <u>deserving</u>
You are ***beautiful***

You are full of **soul**
but always represent *sadness*.
I could repeat these to you, over and over.
They won't fulfill any meaning
until you're strong, amazing, deserving, and beautiful.
Be the soul you're afraid to be.

You will lose *good people*,
good things,
focusing on what no longer matters,
open your eyes.

Rushing things will not make your life speed up faster to where you need to be. You can't rush **love**, *connections*, or careers. If you weren't meant to love someone or something, *it wouldn't be hard* to be patient and enjoy your time when you have it.

Live in the moment. Each moment is another surprise; you can't dictate your life before it happens. You're wasting the time of your life you'll never receive back. *Love what you have when you have it*; everything else will appear on time.

I tried to tell everyone, including myself, that I was done and that love doesn't live within me anymore. Love no longer had a place in my heart. I tried to tell myself I was done; why strive to keep something only I care enough to keep. To think, when you promised we would make it through whatever, you should have promised me you'd never change. That's when I learned when someone makes a promise, they make it for the moment and break it when something better comes along. I'm starting to forget how much the truth hurts because all I receive are lies. Never let a lie make me a fool, even if the truth will kill me. I want so much more than I know I will ever get, and that's when I concluded,

love doesn't live here anymore, **all because of you**.

Never apologize for how you feel.
You're capable of feeling so much.
Feeling **love**, *pain*, **happiness**, and <u>heartbreak</u>.

We've all been **broken**,
some still are.
I know how it feels to be broken
from all the pieces
I learned to love myself.

The energy I surround myself with is no longer weighing me down. It took me a while to realize how **toxic** it was and the love I was afraid to leave behind. The memories I never wanted to forget. *I was selfish with my heart* for people who didn't care to return the same love.

I wish I didn't need to choose,
my pride,
or **you**.

It took years to understand the more I repeated the same ways; *love was never enough*. Their love for me was only as honest as they led me to believe. It's hard to see the toxicity in people when they've been in your life for so long. I've accepted things happen, regardless of whether we know why.

There's *no shame in my love*
No shame in my heart
for the ones I lost.
I have no shame
for the ones *who left me to pick up the pieces.*
Each piece
led me to where I am today.
I thank you,
from the bottom of my heart,
for helping me find myself.
But do me a favor,
stay away from me.

A message to anyone learning to love someone

Self-love doesn't come easy; learning to love yourself is just as challenging as loving others but more intensely. Loving yourself is so important. Every company you keep until you do won't be fully conditioned. When you have people around who help you grow, the ones who help you find you, those are the ones you keep around. You need to surround yourself with those who want to see you win just as much as you do. The more you involve yourself with people who half love you, fake love you, and who give you conditional love, the further away you will feel from yourself. You need to get rid of the people who don't want to see you win. Get rid of those who **love you in the dark** while supporting people they hate in public. This is not the generation of people with pure hearts. People would rather waste time giving you fake love while letting you give them your heart. Don't let these people in your life for any reason; they'll make your journey a longer road. It's essential to protect your aura from people who drain your energy and heart from loving people with good hearts Don't let the demons of your journey bring you to fear in accepting the truth in who you are, where you want to be, and where you're at now. Trust the energy you give, and you will receive that exact in return. Love the ones who love you back unconditionally. Keep the real ones close while you let the ones who drown your soul of sadness and hatred in the dark. Let them go. Be who you want to be. Don't let anyone tell you who you should be; the way you wear your heart on your sleeve is so beautiful. I promise **falling in love with yourself** is just as beautiful, while having people who love you close is like having the *whole moon in your hands*, incredible.

Know your worth,

Make them treat you exactly that,
Anything less isn't worth your energy.

You can't make someone see the good in you, no matter how hard you try. People will see you how they see you, regardless of what you feel. Nothing you ever do will make someone realize your true worth. You don't need to make them aware of your worth. Don't fight for them or their acceptance. They don't care enough to **love you for who you are**, so stop loving them for who they aren't.
They don't deserve you.

Don't be afraid to be free, to be freely who you are.

If you haven't found who that is, don't be discouraged to stop your journey to self-love because you're not clear on where you're at or where you're going. Live your life intensely to the point you don't have time to think about analyzing every situation and decision. Be **fearless** and take on all your fears, weaknesses, and everything that allows you to love yourself fully. Let go of people who don't serve you the way your soul needs. The journey isn't easy; you don't need to have it all figured out; that's the beauty of life, not knowing what could happen and still hoping to have it all figured out. It takes some people forever to love themselves, and some may never understand how important that love is; my heart goes out to all of you. I hope this message can somehow help you understand that your impossible is possible. Everything you want is well deserved if you go and get it. If you love it deeply and love yourself fiercely. Some days you may hate yourself, some days, you'll be obsessed with yourself, and some days you'll just be confused. Understand this is how it all works; you were meant to feel everything you go through. The greatest one of all will be when you **fall in love with yourself**.

Don't settle for what you think you deserve, don't just **settle for love**. Love isn't waking up one day, and the one you love doesn't love you anymore; that's far from love. When you love someone that intimately, you will feel it forever; in this story, forever does exist. Love will always be there, and if they say it wasn't, it never was. You can't wake up and not love someone anymore, but it's possible to outgrow people, change happens, but that love will always remain. You will meet people throughout your life that you will believe you love but won't love. If you ever woke up and thought it could be possible not to love them, it's not love you feel. **People with big hearts** always get confused; that's why it's vital to protect your heart from those who want you when they want you, then get rid of you when they don't need you. It's easy for them, but a person like you, with a big heart, *will scar your heart forever*.

Beauty is so much more than just how people see you. *Your strength is beauty*. The way you love with all your soul, that's beauty. Loving yourself first and letting everything else fall in place. Some might not understand you because they're too busy *seeing beauty through their eyes and not their heart*.

I **wanted** you,
at the time,
I thought I needed you,
I was **blinded** by what I thought love was
and it was making me a fool.

Everyone has that one thing
that makes them *who they are.*
That one thing can't be explained, only **felt**.

The bridges you burnt can't be rebuilt on the same trust and same love that created them. When you decided to burn that bridge, you decided to let go of what was holding it together; the **pain**, the *one-way love*, and the **hope**. You were right to let go, **don't rekindle old flames**.

Since we're being honest,
I never really loved you,
I only **lusted** you.

I found myself letting go of the people I loved most when I realized we weren't on the same path. I realized I couldn't grow with someone who only stunted my growth. I wouldn't say it was toxic, exactly. I would describe it as *no longer pretending their love for me was honest.*

Someone right now doesn't love themselves as you do; **please be kind to them**. Let them know they're not alone. Don't ever judge someone based on only what they show you; there's so much more to someone than what you see on the outside. Their heart is bleeding with the want of being loved, the kind of love you can only receive from yourself. Keep them in mind; keep them close to your heart. It's a mess trying to love yourself in a world of constant reminders of how you can fail at any time.

Love yourself more than those constant reminders.

The thing about people with **good hearts**,

we care too much.
We get upset over the little things
because everything we feel is real.
I've accepted,
I can't change what's not meant to be
, and my heart never will change.
I just trust **karma** to do its thing.

I'm not who I recognize,
I grew into the soul I was meant to be.
I'm still a *work in progress,*
I no longer accept less than I deserve
and some will never understand
why *I had to let them go* to **save me**.

Don't let *old pain*, **old friends**, and *old flames* cloud your mind and make you believe it was your fault you're no longer a part of their life. They couldn't see the real in you; their heart wasn't as they made it seem, and that's not your fault.

There are people out there,
no matter how much you love them,
your love will never be enough.
As sad as it sounds,
they'll never support you
because **it's you**.

I'm not using all my **energy** to hate someone
I once trusted, loved, and chose to have around me.
If we no longer communicate, I still wish you the best.
I pray you find your way,
I'm not going to hold negative energy around me,
you receive what you give.

You can't make someone see the good in you; you can't make someone love you no matter how much they mean to you. That's why it's essential to know your worth; you'll lose yourself trying to *save connections* with people who want to show the world you're not good enough.

People will speak on your name so *shamelessly* but forget to speak on the pain they brought to you and the reciprocated **toxicity** of their character. As if they forgot *they're the reason they view you with so much pain.*

The first step is *finding comfort in yourself* and being able to be alone. You need to find comfort in not needing someone, especially to make you happy. Happiness from everyone will only be temporary until you can be **happy within**. Moving on from someone you love deeply is hard; it could take some time, but if you follow the signs, if you open your eyes and see what's in front of you, you'll be able to go on. Your heart isn't broken; it might seem hard to breathe, but sometimes our hearts are preparing for heartbreak, but heartbreak feels so much worse. Overthinking about letting go can break your own heart. Don't overthink; only make decisions on what's real and what's right there. *Focus on yourself*, and realize your worth before you love someone else, or nothing will make sense.

Don't be discouraged because you *haven't got to where you want to be*; you live your life in your timing and no one else's. So **don't rush good things**; the best things in life come to you when you're not living up to everyone's standards.

There's nothing *wrong with your heart,*
Sometimes it doesn't understand the **first** time.

You can't **keep allowing things** that only bring you *pain*. Stop repeating the same things that keep draining you; you can't blame them for hurting you if you keep letting them. Take responsibility for letting them drain you, accept it, then *let them go*.

Be **thankful** every day you wake up and see another day; whether your day ends with a smile or your day ends in tears, don't end it without being thankful. Thankful for being able to feel every emotion you have been given. Having a heart of gold, a heart that doesn't let you look at things differently, even if it's been hurt. *Always be thankful for being alive even if you don't feel alive.*

I don't care whether I **stand out** or *fit in,*
that never crosses my mind.
If it *sets my soul on fire,*
It's mine.

I found myself attaching **comfort** to my spirit
when I started letting go of
tainted love
and setting free ones
who made love hard to come by.

Know what kind of love you receive by loving yourself first. Every company you keep after will make sense. You'll stop accepting less than you deserve. You won't allow half-love from incomplete people. You won't tolerate disrespect from people who don't know you.

Loving yourself will make you **untouchable**,
It all starts with you.

Find what makes you **happy**,
Make it your life.
Don't ever let go of anything
that *fills your soul*
or what makes you feel **alive**.

Focus on yourself
and loving every part of you.
You'll be able to love another
with the **same love**,
you give yourself.

A message to a **lost** soul:

Don't worry why you haven't got to where you want to be already got to where you are. You can't expect to get everything you dreamed of without working for it. So do whatever you need to accomplish that dream. Some days will be more stressful than others, and some weeks will take forever to end. Some may pass so quickly that you won't remember every detail.

Life is crazy; it's also exciting.

You are life; you are **free**.

You deserve everything you set your mind to and let your heart make your biggest dreams come true. Don't ever get comfortable but always have the comfort you will make it and always find a way. As lost as you may feel now, you'll realize that you always knew who you were; you were just too comfortable and never pushed yourself to your entire self.

You are like *the moon in the night sky*, **beautiful** and unreadable. There's nothing wrong with being a **mystery** to the world *as long as you never lose yourself.*

You will always be the **bad person** in someone else's storyline. I let them put me on that pedestal many times; I let them pick me apart to the point I believed them. There's only so much they can come up with before their *true colors showcase their truth.*

I love looking back to where I was
And see, I **grew**.
Everything I deserved,
I now have it.
Everything I prayed for,
I have received it.
Everything meant to be
Is still processing.
I'm blessed to be living my best life
Even though the downfalls.
I call it *balance*.

People will *love you for everything you aren't* before they love you for everything you are. They'll make you into this idea and attach it to that. There's no love there; that's why it's important to love yourself.

People want you **authentic**,
yet *hate everything*
that makes you different.

You deserve someone honest with you, who will tell you how they feel. Not someone who will wait for you to find out, then try picking up the pieces; that's not love. Love isn't waking up one day and finding out the one you love doesn't love you anymore.

Protect your heart.

Everyone you meet has a purpose in your life; *let them show their purpose.* You'll need them regardless if you think so. Not everyone you meet will be in your life forever; that's where you go wrong. Make sure you learned the lesson they were around to teach you.

You can be the greatest friend in the world
but don't exhaust yourself from trying to save someone
from themselves. You can **listen** to their problems, but it's
not your job to **solve** them.
  That doesn't mean you're not a good friend.

I'm not around to be a **one-sided** friend. I look out for you; I expect you to look out for me. This goes for checking up too, if I'm the only one reaching out, there will come a time when the energy won't be reciprocated, but the *love will always remain.*

You can be the best person in the world, but *you will always be wrong* to someone **who wasn't meant to be in your life**. You can't make someone see the best in you, just like you can't force who's not meant to be in your life.

There are people out there that won't ever be good to you;
they weren't meant to do good by you.
You can't force paths with someone
not meant to be in your life.
Fate is real,
even if you don't believe it.
Doesn't change what's not meant for you.

I find beauty in the things that others find abnormal; I find peace in not trying to fit in or stand out. I found comfort in being myself; that's when I understood my true beauty couldn't be seen, which makes sense why some may never understand me.

If someone shares their **dreams**, **secrets**, and *fears* with you. Please don't use it against them when you're no longer in good company. They loved you enough to tell you the deepest and rawest parts they didn't share with the world; *they found comfort in you.*

Some people may never understand why you had to **let them go**. They won't ever understand why they made you let them go or how they caused you so much pain. Some people just don't get it; *nothing ever is their fault*.

The kind of love you give me
Is the kind of love,
I want to surround my heart for eternity.

The kind of love
I won't ever find it in someone else.
The kind of love
That makes me feel secure.

This is the love I've prayed for.

You **needed** me,
More than I needed you.
I gave all of me for your need,
Yet I'm the **damaged** one.
The one who's always made out to be
The lost one.

Under no obligation was *I meant to fix you*,
that didn't mean I didn't try.
I found myself almost **broken**
trying to mend together
what *wasn't my heartache to recover*.

I found **beauty**
when *I found myself.*

You found your **greatest superpower**
the moment you found yourself.
There's *magic in loving yourself* like no one can.

Don't be afraid to let go of who serves your soul no more purpose. People take a different path and expect you always to follow. *Don't use love as an excuse* to keep unwanted company around your soul.

You **inspire** people who never met you,
and people who love you.
There's no one you inspire more
than the ones *who pretend they don't see you.*

You need to *live intensely* to the point you can feel the same love every time you look at a picture that holds a memory. You won't relive a moment twice, but you will feel it. So don't waste your time trying to relive moments; that's our hearts' job.

There will be people who will **critique** you, *judge you*, and have this wild assumption of who they see you be without letting themselves see how pure your heart is. There will be people who, no matter how good you are to them, *you'll never be good enough*.

If someone gave up on you, don't go back and try rekindling things. Let go the first time. They'll keep you around just to mold you into someone they want you to be. Loving you under their conditions.

What you **feel**, what you *need*, won't matter.

I don't do *half love*, half **friendships**, *half anything*.
I like my things as complete as they come. So I'm not
going to waste my time loving someone who only loves me
when it's convenient for them, or they make it seem as if
they don't love me at all.

Love is only as powerful as you make it. Some you thought you would love forever without putting into perspective that people change; they grow into someone you won't identify. *Love will always remain* but in a way that no longer makes sense.

I believe in not leaving things on bad terms,
but there comes a time
when *no answer is where you'll find comfort.*

It's sad to know one day you **outgrow** people,
after realizing how difficult it was
trying to make something fit
that grew out of place.

There are good people out there who will always love you unconditionally for who you are. These people will inspire you. They're called soulmates. You don't always get to keep them, so cherish them when they're around. Some people will come around to blind you into believing they love you when they don't.

It's always a choice,
you either *grow together*,
or you **outgrow** them.

Happiness comes from within.
If you can't find it within yourself,
I promise you,
you won't find it in anyone else.
You'll ruin yourself
trying to find happiness in places it doesn't exist.

You shouldn't need to **explain** who you are to anyone.
If they don't value you without explanation,
they *don't deserve you*.

We *fall in love with moments*,
In hopes that not one thing changes.
Suddenly you realize,
people **grow**
and you're supposed to love them the same.

To **love yourself** completely,

you need to let go of the things that don't love you back.
Once you stop loving things that don't give any value to
you, you'll have the energy to love yourself
wholeheartedly.

My **intuition** has always brought light to every situation. Being able to sense the outcome of someone's actions before they even show me. Always trust every vibe you get; there's too much real love out there to be wasting your time on someone who only *loves you in the dark*.

If it makes you happy,
don't worry about what anyone says.
Miserable people
have miserable minds,
don't let them drown you.

You're **not hard to love**,
you just don't love with limitations.
You love,
with all your soul or not at all.
Don't take half love from the ones
you give your whole heart to.

I *never had the desire to fit in,*
I was perfectly made to be authentic.
I don't need to stand out to prove it,
I never accepted the opinions
When everyone tried to make me believe
I was a copy.

When they were just upset
I loved myself more than their judgment.

I loved people
even after they showed me I shouldn't.
There's nothing **deceptive** about me.

There's so much good
that comes from **pain**,
like finding out
someone no longer deserves your energy.

You grow up learning,
how to **treat others**,
how to *make friends*,
how to **love others unconditionally**.
All these years
you grow up learning,
while the most important lesson in life,
learning to love yourself.
Why does it take years to learn that?

Don't ever settle for **comfort**.
You'll never get what you deserve,
giving yourself only what comforts you
Instead of what *makes your soul alive.*

You need to own who you are
and **love** you,
to the point everyone's opinions
will be *noise to your ears*.

Everyone I come across,
will have a version of me they'll run with.
Who I am will always be
unfamiliar,
misunderstood,
and **fixed**.
I come to terms with letting them
run with whatever makes them satisfied.
When it comes down to it,
their version of me is just their **illusion**.

Love isn't blind; at least to me, it's not. I can tell you when I felt love, real love, there was nothing blind about it. I felt it immediately after facing it.

I do agree,

People can let love blind them, using love as an excuse to let no-good people keep **destroying** them.

It's essential to *relive every situation* you have been through, through **memories**, of course. It's essential to take the good and realize how it's helped you grow. Also, take the bad and how it made you into who you are without them. The first step to letting go of toxicity is to understand what about someone makes them toxic. You need to accept you can't change or make someone love you who wasn't meant to love you. They were meant to stop by and teach you they're someone you don't need anyone; they teach you how important being comfortable in your solitude is, getting you ready to love the person you were meant to give your all to. It comes down to you; toxic people can only keep intoxicating you if you let them. Show them you'll always do good without them while **loving yourself** beautifully.

It's so comforting to know you grew apart from the bad and left all the burden behind you. You're looking towards a happier positive life, full of blessings. You'll grow to realize the love you once felt wasn't love; it was a way of getting you ready to love your soulmate, to learn what love is not, and to be able to love wholeheartedly.

Love yourself first, always.

Sometimes you don't know when it's time to walk away until being separated from the situation suits you better than it ever did while you were in it.

I loved myself more than I loved them,
they couldn't accept that.

It's completely ironic,
when I did what I had to do,
to *cut ties that were loose* for some time.
I don't apologize,
for walking away from them.
It was exactly what I needed to grow
but **I will apologize** for the closure,
they'll never get,
because they were too proud to admit
they were the reason.

If someone tells you they can't be with you because of them, believe them. They need to work on them to love you in the ways you deserve. Stop searching for that someone; let them find you. Search for **who you are** and *find who you are before you give your love away.*

You **outgrow** old situations, friendships, and love. Not everyone you connect with will be a lifetime connection. They were meant to go, you can't unlive the times, but you can accept they outlived their time. You outgrow them and decide to *separate your heart from the old.*

I'm not impressed by the heartless; I got too much heart to be cold. Too much love to give to the ones worth my time. If my heart disconnects from you, it doesn't intend to be cold toward you; I just learned to distance my heart from **the love that's no longer desired**.

I no longer have misery in my heart; I let the misery die when I let go of the pain. So I stopped welcoming shady, undesirable connections that only led to disappointments. I've evolved; I became more than who they made me be; *their phony love was the birth of my masterpiece.*

I refuse to listen to the ones who never wanted to see me love myself from the beginning. Ones who only stunted my growth and made me feel like I needed them more. To this day, they swear their intentions were pure but became a **ghost** when *I finally loved myself more.*

I witnessed people speak to someone with the highest amount of disrespect after loving them. Makes me wonder what kind of love they were taught. I've witnessed people explain someone while knowing they were explaining themselves instead, not realizing they were the **toxic ones in the story**.

I started realizing it wasn't only about watching who I let get close to me, but more about who I kept around me and how easy it was for them to *switch up*.

Just because you have a **good heart**,
that doesn't mean
you should give all your love away
because you have enough to give.
Some people don't deserve your love.

When someone shows you their **true colors**, believe them. Don't try to convince yourself otherwise. *Don't wear your heart on your sleeve* when it comes to this; set your heart to the side, and don't be blind.

I *became distant from souls*
I never wanted to be without,
that's when I found **comfort in being alone**.

I don't want to hear that things will get better. I don't want to hear bad things happen so better things can arrive. So when I ask you to listen to me, *I want you to listen*.

I've been guilty of the too-busy card, and I won't deny it. I won't ever deny I didn't text someone for a whole day because I needed to get my thoughts in order. Some days I needed to know what came next, or maybe I needed some space. In every connection, **no one craves company all of the time**; some need it more than others. I hate the feeling I always need to be there, and if I'm not, *I'm a horrible friend*.

Many people
have *too much pride*
To show **a soft side**.

I pray one day you wake up and realize you're more than people make you appear to be. Your beauty is more profound than how people see you. I pray you wake up one day and realize you don't need to impress anyone. You just need to love yourself a little more than you love them.

You put your all into someone you loved,

you were clueless about why you did. When you love intensely, it can get the best of you, and not always in a good way. You let love become a weapon; you become blinded by it. You'll know the difference between the two kinds of love when you realize yourself loving them and not trying your hardest to prove that love. When it's real love, they will feel it as much as you. There are ups and downs, but no one who truly loves you will ever hurt you and make you believe you're someone hard to love. People like us, with big hearts, let love not only be a good drug to us but also let it destroy us. If you never learned what love wasn't, you could never appreciate what love is. You'll never understand the real if you can't compare the fake. Everything you go through in life is a lesson. We need to find the parts of us that are still hidden; we often learn something new about ourselves. You need to accept not everyone is meant for you. Some will only be out to hurt you because that's the role they were meant to play in your life, don't try and change that.

Acknowledge the hate
that's within you,
before you try to love me.
I'm not trying to **save** you,
that will only *destroy* me.
There's no love there.

Josephine Rivera

July 13, 1992 – April 17, 2017

Young Naked Soul

If I asked anyone to explain what YoungNakedSoul meant, they would probably refer to someone being young and naked forgetting the most important part, the soul. When I hear those words I think about you, Josie. Someone who was young and had a naked mindset   one not many understood but loved anyway. A mindset with no limits, you did whatever set your soul on fire, and you lived to the truth of your own life. Naked doesn't always mean being without clothes, anyone can be naked but to be able to share your spirit, fears, dreams, and feelings with someone, that's being naked. You're giving someone the power to destroy you while having faith they won't break you. Who would have thought those three would hold so much meaning?

Missing someone who isn't ever coming back… like impossible? That's true heartbreak. Knowing there's nothing I can do to bring you back breaks me. Sometimes it's hard to breathe. Sometimes it's hard to keep my tears in and sometimes it's hard to even believe this is all real.

I want to thank you for giving me some of the most incredible memories. Thank you so much for blessing my life with your existence. I will forever remember every single memory you gave me. I might not have been close to you enough, maybe you didn't tell me every fear and feeling… but you told me the things you wanted me to know. I'm trying to stop analyzing why God chose you. trying to accept you are now my guardian angel. I'm trying so hard not to be broken when all I want to do is break down. It's harder because your soul was so pure, you touched everyone you knew.

It's just so hard not knowing how to feel, you become numb to everything. It hurts. It hurts because you told me on **June 22, 2016**: *"I will never never leave you, I promise"* but you're gone and I know this wasn't your plan; you wouldn't have left me. I will forever be broken in hopes of seeing you again, and for my broken heart to be healed.

All I'm left with now are memories that will forever be with me. I won't ever forget your smile. I miss you so much. So yes, those three words always remind me of you. those three words mean more to me than they will to anyone I try and explain them to.

It's **August 20, 2017,** to be exact. The last time I wrote was Mat 1, 2017. I couldn't seem to find the words, or process the thoughts to make a whole feeling. I'm feeling you a little different today. I started this thing where I'm no longer just writing for me, I'm writing for you too because I know you hear me and feel me. I know you understand me. I know you're smiling at me telling me to keep being amazing. I couldn't be happier to have someone like you watching over me, I feel you so deeply. The feeling is so crazy, like a high I don't ever want to come down from like I won't understand why you had to be taken so soon. I feel like everything that was once there had gone with you like it's lost and I'm trying to find it. That feeling is so powerful and so heartbreaking. Only you can feel me, no one else can feel me.

I never understood death. I never coped with it, I have a habit of pushing things behind me so I don't need to deal with the pain. Sometimes we change for the better and sometimes we change according to the situation, and sometimes we don't change for the better.

I taught myself not to feel. My grandparents passed I was wrecked but I ended up shifting that pain into the back of my heart because I thought not feeling would help me cope with it. instead, every time I thought of them I had tears. I didn't let myself feel these levels of emotions and explore them to heal through them. I didn't understand the impact death had on the heart. I didn't understand what it meant to feel and the healing in it. I taught myself not to understand the importance of having a heart. I was heartless in a way but my heart was always there under the darkness. You go through so much and don't come out the same. *Heartbreak changes you.*

I always replay memories and thoughts because I want to remember everything and relive that moment over and over. I don't ever want to forget you. I don't ever want to forget what you meant to me. I can still remember your smile and the exact image in my head is so genuine. I learned what it was like to be broken and feel like you're no longer whole. I learned what it felt like to have your heart ripped right out of your chest and slammed back in because well, people with good hearts always come out strong; that's what you taught me. you showed me what it's like to feel. You showed me how much a person could feel and how there's no limit. The more you feel the stronger you become. So I no longer care when people tell me to stop being emotional.

I wish this were all a terrible nightmare. Sometimes I drown in the thought of being without you. Sometimes I feel like you were never gone but I know I need to accept it and know the reality, that you're in spirit and not whole. You will always be the greatest friend who blessed me with the greatest life lesson. Showing me what it's like to be myself completely, to not be afraid to feel. To love deeply. You made it so easy to love you just by being you.

I want to thank everyone who supported me throughout my journey. Over the years I wrote many pieces I haven't shown to the world, I can't tell you how amazing it feels to publish my own story. I never listened to those who shamed me and didn't think I could make it. writing is my therapy and it completes me in every way.

It's hard to walk a journey without a map of where I'll end up but 2017 taught me that people change and when it's time to move on, let go. Sometimes the only one you have is yourself. I learned to love people from afar. I learned to love myself through all of this. I hope my book helps you understand yourself in a way you won't need the approval of others. I hope my book makes you feel as beautiful as you deserve. I hope you all stick around and love everything I send your way, even if you don't always relate. I'm your friend. Knowing someone else needed to hear my story brings me so much peace.

All my platforms:

Instagram: Moonsoulchild
Twitter: Bymoonsoulchild
Tiktok: Bymoonsoulchild
Facebook: Moonsoulchild
Apple Music: Moonsoulchild
Spotify: Moonsoulchild

Moonsoulchild.com

Made in the USA
Las Vegas, NV
16 November 2022

59618988R00105